Sometimes

Samantha Taylor

BookLeaf Publishing

India | USA | UK

Presentation by *BookLeaf Publishing*

Web: www.bookleafpub.com

E-mail: info@bookleafpub.com

ISBN : 9789357448420

First edition 2021

DEDICATION

Dedicated to Polly, my little sister and to all the kids past, present and future that I work with.

You inspire me every day to do better and be better!

ACKNOWLEDGEMENT

I'd like to acknowledge my partner Alex, who let me use her paypal to sign up for this challenge... and supports me in everything I do. No matter how big, how small or how bizarre.

PREFACE

Okay so I'd like to preface this by saying I am very aware that I am NOT a poet. Please don't bully me lol

Sometimes

Feelings can be confusing
If you're big
Or if you're small
But sometimes I think sadness
is the most confusing
of all

Sometimes it will come and go
like the breeze it doesn't stay
sometimes it hurts so much
it stays around all day

Sometimes I don't even realise
sadness is close by
like in the seconds before I lose something
or fail even when I try

Sadness can also trick me
into thinking things that aren't true
like I'll never be good at anything
no matter what I do

Sadness can overwhelm me
turn things I love into a chore
suddenly, things I used to love to do

I don't want to do anymore

I know sometimes there is a reason
like if someone I love leaves, or if I fall
But sometimes, sadness is just there
for no reason at all

All I know is that when I feel it
It is best to acknowledge it, say "hello!"
Because if I try to ignore it
I don't think it will ever go

So, whenever sadness is close by
I'll find someone I trust, let them know
I'll hold them tight
they'll hold me
and we'll both hold on to tomorrow

Polly

Little hands, little feet
A face so tender, so sweet

How could I ever forget the day
My life changed, in every way?

Little fingers, little nose
Little legs squeezed into little clothes

From now until the very end
you are my little sister, my best friend

Learning to talk, learning to walk
learning to dance, learning to sing
my little sister, my everything

So little sister, as you grow
I hope no matter what, you always know
That I am here, and I stay
holding your hand, every step of the way

Little hands, little feet
Tiny heartbeat
So precious, so small

My life has meaning after all

Alex

Warm sun
Cold breeze
My ladybird
Amongst the bees

Returning home
After being away too long
The favourite part
Of my favourite song

Warm bath
Lots of bubbles
Cold night
Filled with cuddles

My sunflower
In a field full of thorns
A beautiful rainbow
In the middle of storms

Comfort
I don't think I've known
Finally
My heart is home

Grandma Rose

Christmas around the table
Everyone I knew
I cared about the presents
But should have spent more time
With you

I never got to know
If you were someone who enjoyed the snow
So, when Christmas comes each year
I wish that you were still here

Across the world
Across the sea
It no longer snows on Christmas Eve
It's too hot at night to sleep
I wonder if you would prefer this heat

Each year, the magic
Seems to dim
No matter what, Santa
May bring
But the thought of you
On Christmas day
Is enough to remind me
I'll be okay

Joking around the Christmas tree
I wonder if you'd think I'm funny
Would you be proud of who I am today?
I lie awake, Imagining
What you might say

I'm not one for believing
I don't know if you were too
But I like to think
My guiding star is you

And each year, the magic
Seems to dim
No matter what Santa
May bring
But when I'm lost
When I can't find my way
I think of you at the table
On Christmas day

Glitter

Glitter
Thrown all through your hair
Glitter
Still scattered everywhere

Glitter
Will always remind me of you
You shined so bright
Regardless of what you were going through

Glitter is what you leave behind
Glorious specs of happiness
In everybody's mind

I know there are many
That would say the same
That we'll think of glitter
When we hear your name

I hope that now you can see
That your glitter
Even spread to me

Glitter

Thrown all through your hair
Your love, your warmth
Still scattered everywhere

Dear, Younger Me

Hello there Younger Me
I'm sure you have lots of questions
Most of them probably about Glee
No you never did marry Naya Rivera
Don't ask anymore about that
You won't want to know the answer

You never become an actress
But don't freak it's okay
You actually work with children
And you smile every day

Some things you find aren't meant for you
But that doesn't mean you fail
Everyone has different journeys
Different times their ships set sail

You never do quite figure out
How to fix your right eyebrow
That thing never grows in right
But you've come to terms with it now

You get quite sick soon
A sickness that doesn't go away
It's hard, I won't lie

It affects you every day

You lie awake a lot of nights
Scared that you love differently
But as you grow, so do others
And you're proud, just wait and see

You have your own little home now
It has a big purple front door
And the things you once worried about
Don't eat away at you anymore

It is filled with trinkets and music
And LOTS of rainbow
I promise things will be alright
I'm you, I know

So, I may not be the person
You dreamed that we would be
But trust me when I say
The most important thing is, we're happy

Dad

You use string to tighten the slack
Around your pants
But we still see your bum crack

I got you a belt, on fathers day
To stop them falling
But they still find a way

When not at work, you're in your shed
Fixing something
While the wind blows that one hair on your head

You pat down your cargo pants, to locate your
wallet
Just to soon realise
That you've forgot it

Without fail, we always know
Wherever you're walking
You'll stub a toe

A chef, I'm afraid you will never be
You made me curry with chicken nuggets
... Really?

You sniff, sing and whistle out of the blue
They say daughters become their mothers
But I think I'm turning into you

I Knew a Girl

I knew a girl
Whose eyes were like the sea
They weren't blue
But they were drowning me

I knew a girl, I adored
But she couldn't feel the same
A girl that left
Just as quickly as she came

She was a girl, whose laugh
Was the sound of my happiness
I fell for her, and all of her messiness

Shoes

Nothing beats a good pair of shoes
The only hard thing
Is knowing which pair to choose

I have my white ones, my whiter ones
My whiteish ones and my newer ones
My older ones, my oldest ones
And my newest ones

I find that my shoes say a lot about my day
My whiteish, older ones say
"Hey... I guess I'm doing okay."

My whiter, newest ones let everyone know
"I am the coolest,
No matter where I go"

I have ones that I don't really care much about
Like my work ones, my slippers
And the ones I wear to take the bins out

I've heard there's a saying
That we should all try
Walk in someone else's shoes

But I think I'd rather die

How do people write poems?

How do people write those poems?
You know, the ones that don't rhyme?
I don't understand how to do that
I tried doing that with mine
They didn't turn out so great
In fact they were all bad
I tried everything I could
I gave it all I had
This is the end result
And obviously, I failed
Unless...
I just stop rhyming now?
Like...
What if i just
Bailed?

Dammit.

Adults?

I have a friend named Maddy
She legit OWNS a home
I have a friend named Emily
She legit LIVES on her own
But I, Sammy
Still haven't paid off my phone

Friends that I grew up with
Actually have children now
Yet I still can't look after
Myself, somehow

We all seem to be making things up
As we go along
Guessing and trying
But still getting it wrong

Why does my car
Need SO many coloured slips?
I still don't know who to call
When my kitchen tap constantly drips

I forget my washing in the washer
Or forget it's on the line
There's actually a wasp nest next to it

But I'll just ignore it, I'm sure it will be fine

And maybe, juuuust maybe, one day
I won't snooze my alarm
But for now, an extra ten minutes
Won't do any harm

Forbidden Fruit

Forbidden fruit
I want to take my shot
But I can't shoot

My hands are shackled
I can't take a bite
We both know
This isn't right

I can hold your hand in mine
But I can't bring you to my lips
I think about you all the time
But I can't act on it

When we dance
And you pull me close
That's when I miss you
The most

I have to turn away
What will people say?
Forbidden fruit
Forbidden fruit

I have you in my sights

You're lined up in my aim
We can't help how we feel
We're not the ones to blame
I just hope one day
We won't have to
Run away
We know it's not wrong
We've known it all along

So I'm gonna hold you in my arms
I'm going to bring you to my lips
I think about you all the time
I'm going to act on it

Forbidden fruit
I'm going to take my shot
It's time to shoot

Unicorns

If the cat meows
And the cow goes moo
What on earth
Would a unicorn do?

If a dog goes woof
And a horse goes neigh
What on earth
Would a unicorn say?

If a pig oinks
And sheep go baaaaa
I think that unicorns would say
"yaaas, lady gagaaaa"

Anywhere I Go

Your hairs still in the shower
Towel, still on the rack
I know that this time
You're not coming back

Your hair ties and your perfume
Still scattered around my room
Your cup from your last drink
Toothbrush, left by the sink
A footprint at the door
That I don't see you stood at anymore

So anywhere I go
Anything I do
I turn around
And I see you

The End

This is it now
Finally closed the book
I know it's over now
You can't pass me a second look

Finished the last chapter
Nothing more to write
I know it's over now
We've had our final fight

There are no more pages to turn
All the bridges we built are burned
You got what you wanted
Not me
So I guess we've reached the end
Of our story

The pages are torn
The cover is worn
You've put down the pen
It's a book I'll never recommend

Because while you're off writing
With someone new
I'm still reading

About you

Mum

I love coming home
To sit on the couch with you
A coffee in our hands
Kettle boiled for two

Watching bake off
And antiques roadshow
While you tell me
Random info
About movie stars and what you've heard about
On the news

How your jaw sticks out
When you're angry
And you have no idea
How to work the T.V
Playing gin rummy
On the floor
While Willow scratches
At the door

Your support with anything
That I try

How you make me laugh
Till I cry

So when I'm down
I come around
We sing a song
And you put the kettle on

And when you're down
I'll come around
Sing you a song
And I'll put that kettle on

Smell The Roses

I don't want to smell the roses
anymore
I don't want to smell the roses
Like I used to before
I don't need your approval
anymore
I've found my way
It's right out the door
I've been cut by thorns
before
But my wounds
Are no longer raw
So after all of the cuts, the scars
and the bruises
You're the one
Who loses

Don't tell me to look on the bright side
I've been in the dark too long
I'm sick of blaming myself
For everything
You did wrong

She Said To Me (Part of a poem I wrote for a mental health awareness concert)

She said to me
if you could see yourself through my eyes
you'd see your brain is telling you lies
but my insides feel so toxic, putrid, ugly
why is it that I think nobody should love me?
She said to me
"you are the strongest person i know"
why do i find that so hard to believe though?
When somebody confides in me about their
mental health
I understand and I listen, why can't I do that
with myself?

I'm not weak for needing a helping hand

I spent so long spiralling I just need some
support to stand
and the days that are so dark and heavy so deep
in my chest
they still happen but I'm trying my best

There's a difference between lonely and alone
because there are people that call me, i just can't
pick up the phone
a tsunami of destruction filling my mind
because a purpose can be so hard to find
and I'm still not sure
what I'm here for
I still have no idea
why I'm here
but right now I'm spilling my heart out on a page
filled with worry, loss, grief and so much rage
because if someone listens and my words echo
through their head
maybe a line or rhyme from my story replays as
you lie in bed
maybe it gives you some sort of comfort to show
you're not alone
in whatever you're feeling, trust me... I know

Or maybe something I've said has given you
some sort of sign
that maybe... Just maybe with a little bit of time
you will realise,

you're never a burden or in the way,
I promise that tomorrow is another day,
there are things worth fighting for
and it is NEVER wrong to want more

She said to me
"Depression is a liar, nothing it says is true
your life has value"
Said to me
that she loved me
and so I'll let her, wholeheartedly

www.ingramcontent.com/pod-product-compliance
Lightning Source LLC
LaVergne TN
LVHW041247200726
843507LV00013B/2857